PMS

Problems Men Started

PMS

Problems Men Started

By Nikki Hardin and Caitilin McPhillips

Illustration and design by Traci Daberko

skirt!®

Guilford, Connecticut

An Imprint of The Globe Pequot Press

10 9 8 7 6 5 4 3 2 1

Printed in China

Text and cover design by Traci Daberko
daberkodesign.com

Library of Congress Cataloging-in-Publication Data
Hardin, Nikki.
PMS {problems men started} / Nikki Hardin and Caitilin McPhillips.
p. cm.
ISBN-13: 978-1-59921-222-7
1. Men—Humor. I. McPhillips, Caitilin. II. Title.
PN6231.M45H334 2008
818.602—dc22

2007006374

skirt!®

skirt!® is an attitude... spirited, independent, outspoken, serious, playful and irreverent, sometimes controversial, always passionate.

We Don't Hate Men.

We love men and one of us is actually married to one. In fact, **PMS** was HIS idea. So please send **him** any hate mail you may be penning at this moment. But before you put a stamp on that letter... Read a few of the entries and think about them. Think about them some more, and laugh a little. Accept that in the past guys might have been a bit quick to start a war, take an extra wife or two, burn some unbelievers at the stake, and lock their wives up in chastity belts. We know that's all water under the bridge, but we're just trying to keep men on their toes in the future. **PMS** is our payback, our answer to Dumb Blonde Jokes, booty calls, and years of last-minute supermarket make-up bouquets.

Nikki Hardin & Caitilin McPhillips

(with special thanks to Kevin McPhillips)

P.S. Remember, it was HIS idea, not ours.

P.P.S. We know you must have your own secret stash of Problems Men Started. Problems that keep you awake at night or make your blood boil while you're in the carpool line. Submit them to us at www.skirt.com and you may see them in a future edition of ***PMS***.

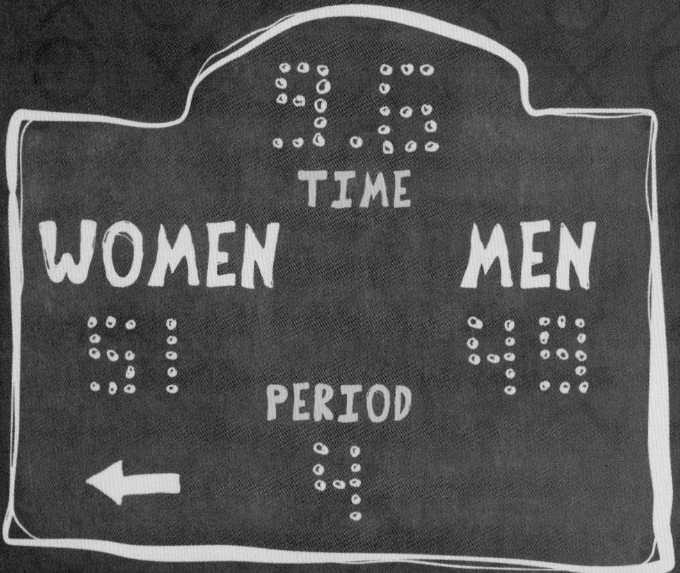
TIME
WOMEN
MEN
PERIOD

QUOTE

"Men play the game;
women know the score."

- Roger Woddis

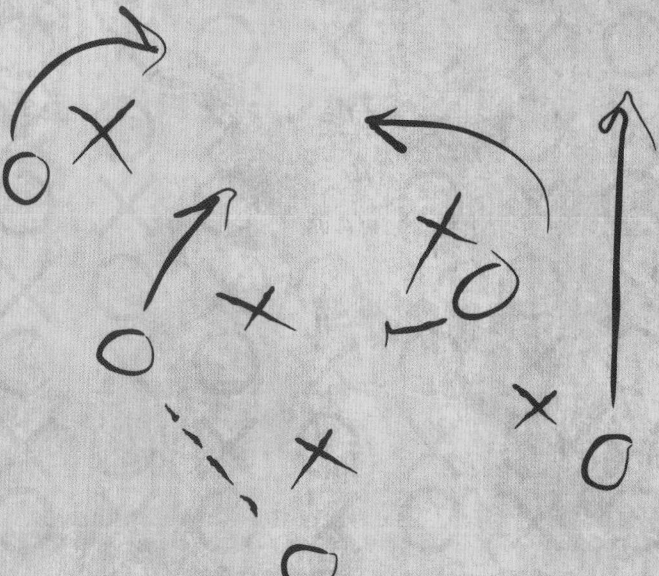

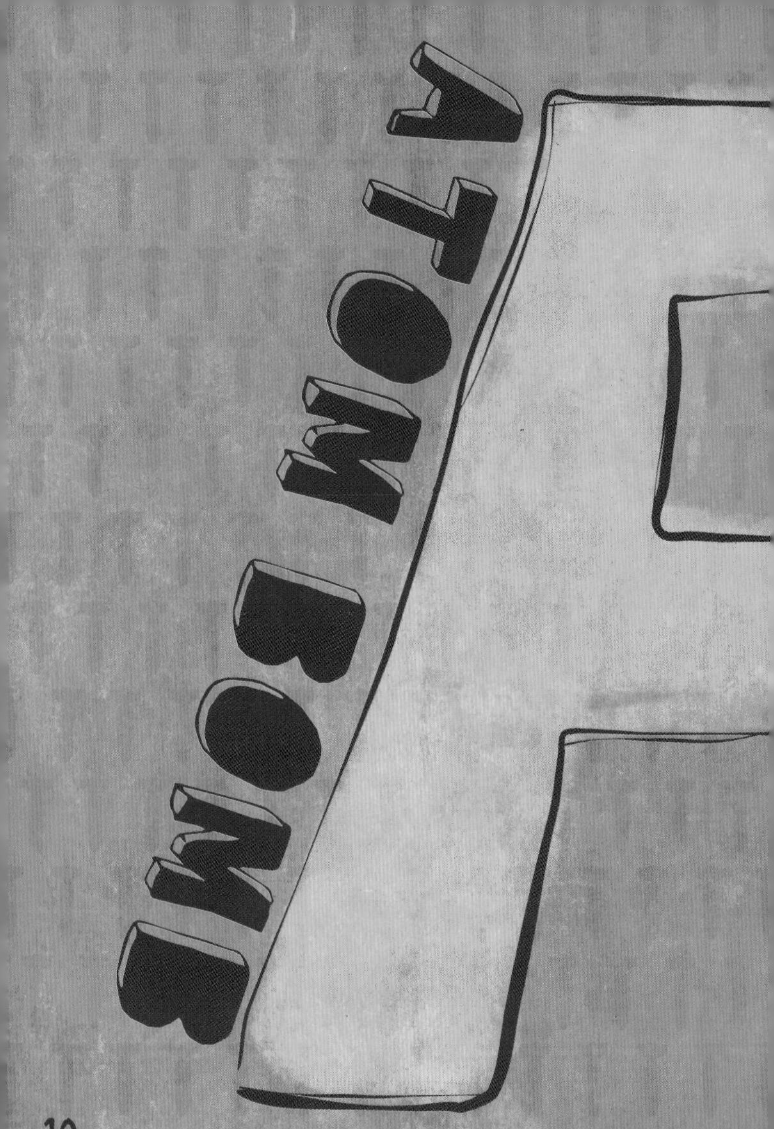
ATOM BOMB

ALGEBRA

CON SPIR ACY THEORIES

The dog ate my homework

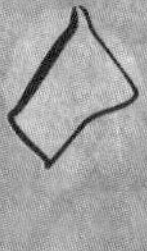

2 MUCH BASS

[Car Stereo Bass Overload]

2 MUCH NOISE

[Bluetooth® Earphones]

2 MANY EMPTY WORDS

[Rush Limbaugh]

DOPPLER RADAR

Cyber-SEX

OIL SPILLS
Overfishing The Oceans
Global Warming

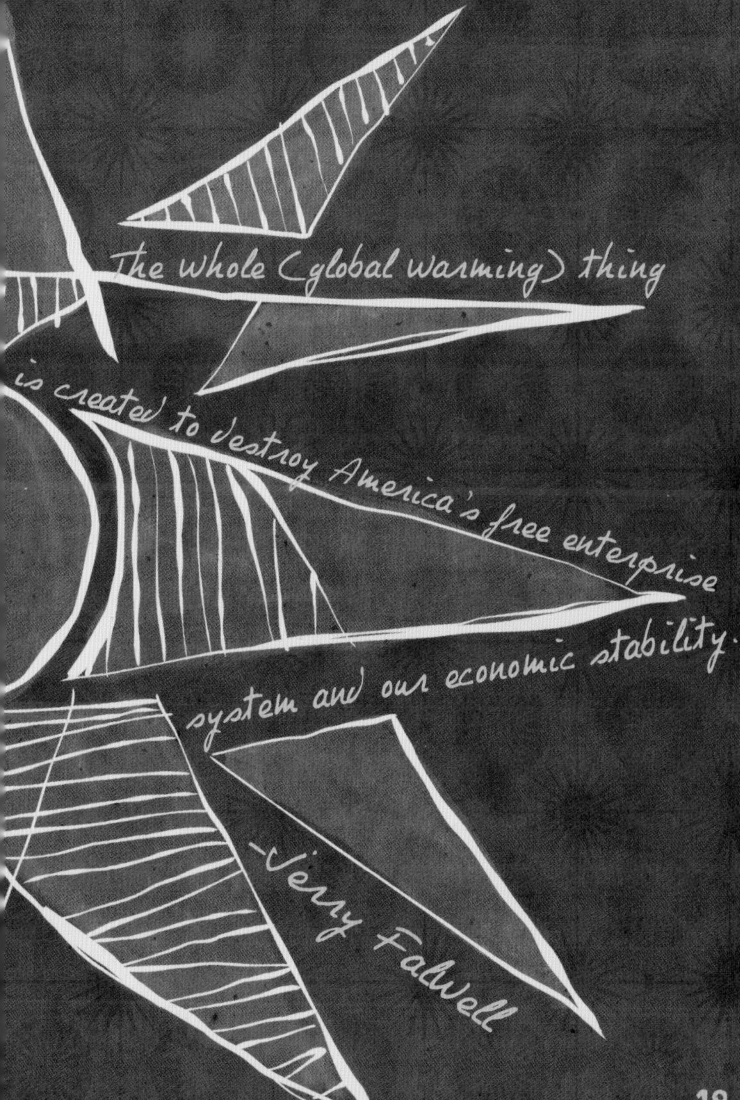
The whole (global warming) thing
is created to destroy America's free enterprise
system and our economic stability.
-Jerry Falwell

Baseball

STRIKES

Q:

How can you tell a FAx has been sent from a blonde?

A:

There's a stamp on it.

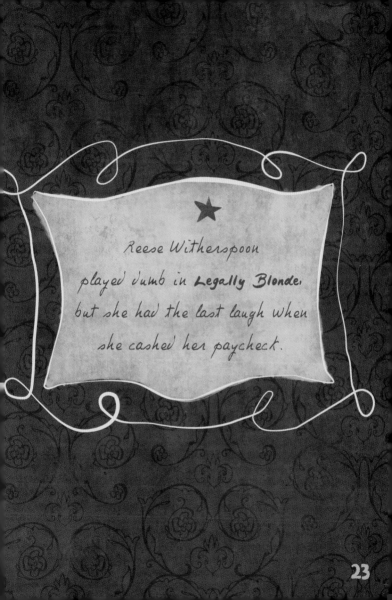

Reese Witherspoon played dumb in **Legally Blonde**, but she had the last laugh when she cashed her paycheck.

SUPER STORES

Sizing SUPER BOWLS

"Most of us are poor. Home and water are all we have. We have no place other than our land to move to. We endure what the coal companies put us through."

Julia Bonds

Coalminer's daughter & environmental activist

STRIP CLUBS

STRIP MINING

Strip Malls

SPAM

Polyester

CALL WAITING
Telemarketers
OBSCENE CALLS

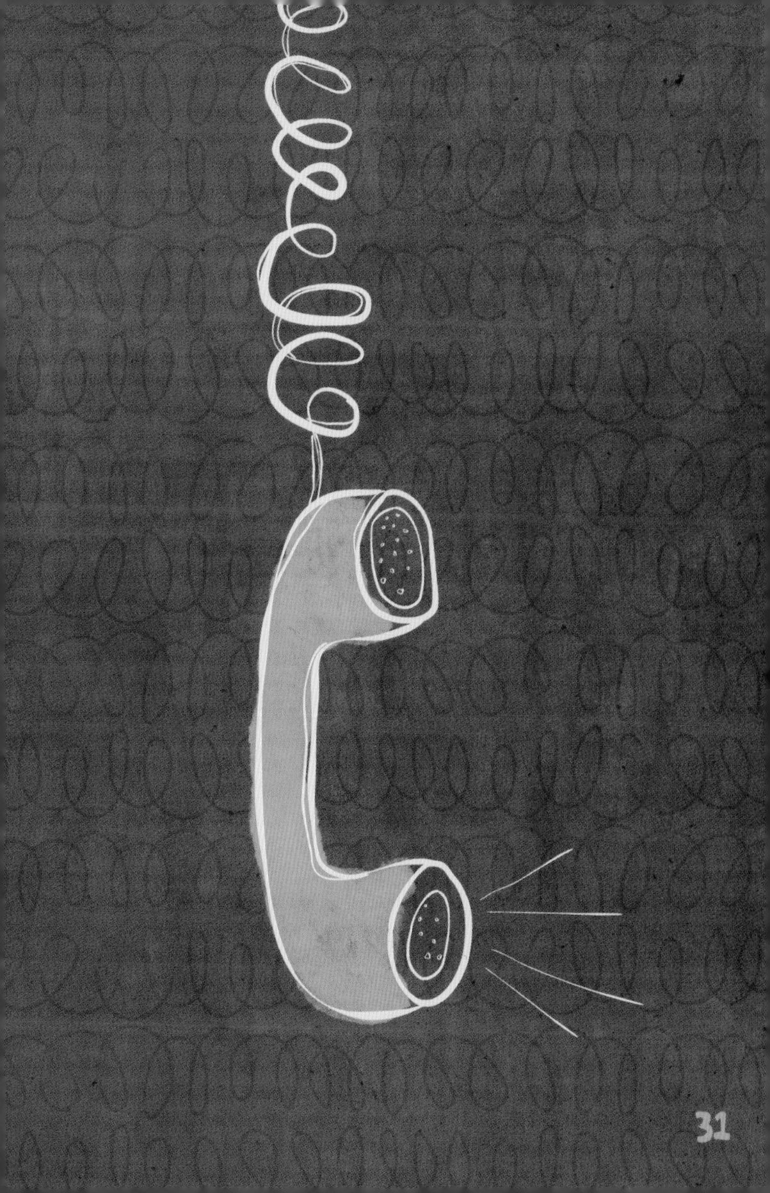

Shaving Legs

SilicOne imPlants

HOO

WOULD YOU LIKE
SOME CHICKEN WITH
THOSE BREASTS?

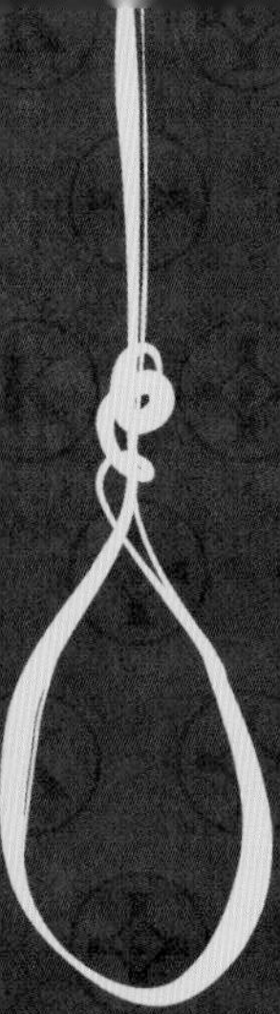

Ku Klux Klan

Custer's Last Stand

FOCUS ON THE FAMILY

QUOTE:

"Briefly stated, love is linked to self-esteem in women. For a man, romantic experiences with his wife are warm and enjoyable and memorable—but not necessary."

-Dr. James Dobson, founder

Pornography

QUOTE:

The interesting thing is how one guy, through living out his own fantasies, is living out the fantasies of so many other people.

-Hugh Hefner

PLAYBOY®

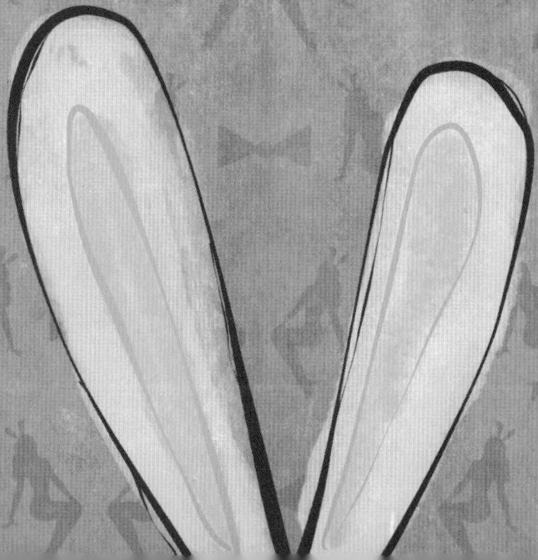

MARATHONS

MEN IN SPEEDOS®

FAST FOOD
TV DINNERS

FAT JOKES
TRANS FATS

"What's your sign?"

PICK-UP

"You must be tired because you've been running through my mind all day."

"I'm not the most attractive guy in here, but I'm the only one talking to you."

LINES

"Should I call you in the morning or just nudge you?"

GLASS

CEILING

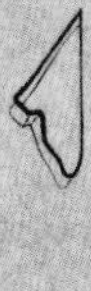

"We aim to give a 'wake-up call' to businesses, to alert them to the fact that the next 'fair-haired boy' of their organization just might be a woman."

–Elizabeth Dole

TROPHY WIVES

EMOTICONS

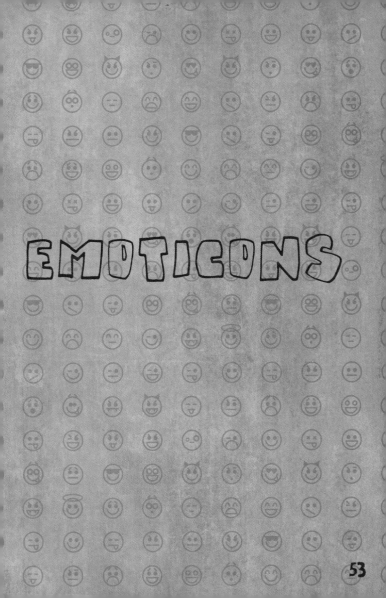

Las Vegas

ASTROTURF®

BARBERSHOP

QUARTETS

HOMOPHOBIA

"The not-like-us ethos makes so much bigotry possible: Racism, sexism, homophobia. It divides the country as surely as the Mason-Dixon line once did. And it makes for mean-spirited and punitive politics and social policy."

—Anna Quindlen

Novelty Condoms

Spanish Inquisition

cockfights

PRENUP Agreements

QUOTE:

"My husband and i didn't sign a prenuptial agreement. We signed a mutual suicide pact." -Roseanne Barr

PROMISE KEEPERS

MYTH:

"The Promise Keepers are good for women."

FACT:

As feminists, we have long urged men to take responsibility in the home, as the Promise Keepers claim to do. However, when they say "taking responsibility" they mean taking control. Promise Keepers openly call for wives to "submit" to their husbands.

NOW (www.now.org)

Scientology

In the late 1940s, pulp writer L. Ron Hubbard declared:

"Writing for a penny a word is ridiculous. If a man really wants to make a million dollars, the best way would be to start his own religion."

Reader's Digest reprint, May 1980, p. 1

Hubbard later created the Church of Scientology...

THE HOLO

CAUST

TANNING BEDS

WATERBEDS

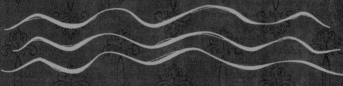

NRA

QUOTE:

"The number of children and teens killed by gun violence in 2003 alone exceeds the number of American fighting men and women killed in hostile action in Iraq from 2003 to 2006." –Children's Defense Fund

CAMOUFLAGE

CLOTHING

Booty Calls

BOOTY-BRUISING BIKE SEATS

THE THIRTY YEARS' WAR
1618-1648

GULF WAR

August 2, 1990 – February 28, 1991

THE CRUSADES
1095-1291

THE HUNDRED YEARS' WAR

1337–1453

Women On a Pedestal

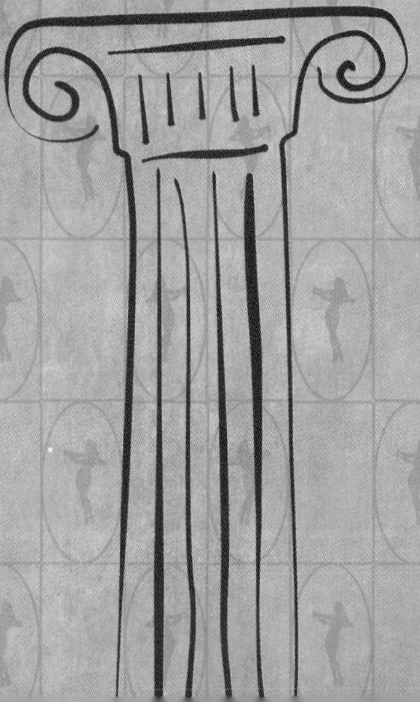

GIRLS GONE WILD

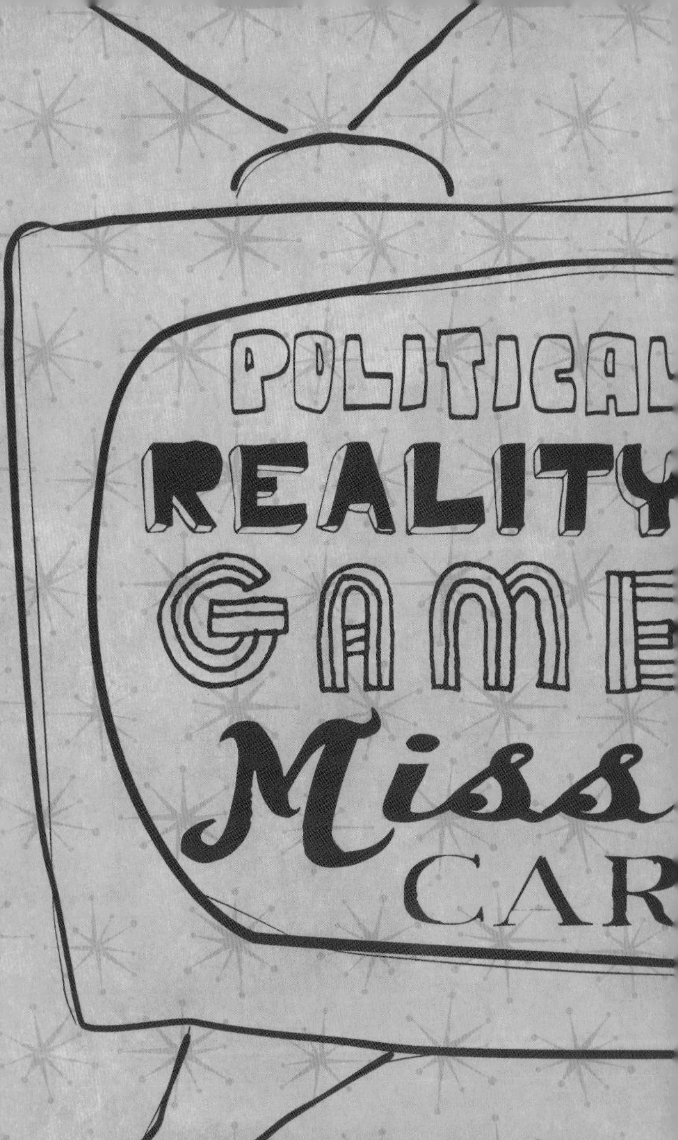
POLITICA
REALITY
GAME
Miss
CAR

ADS
SHOWS
SHOWS
America
COMMERCIALS

CIVIL WAR reenactments

WIFE BEATERS

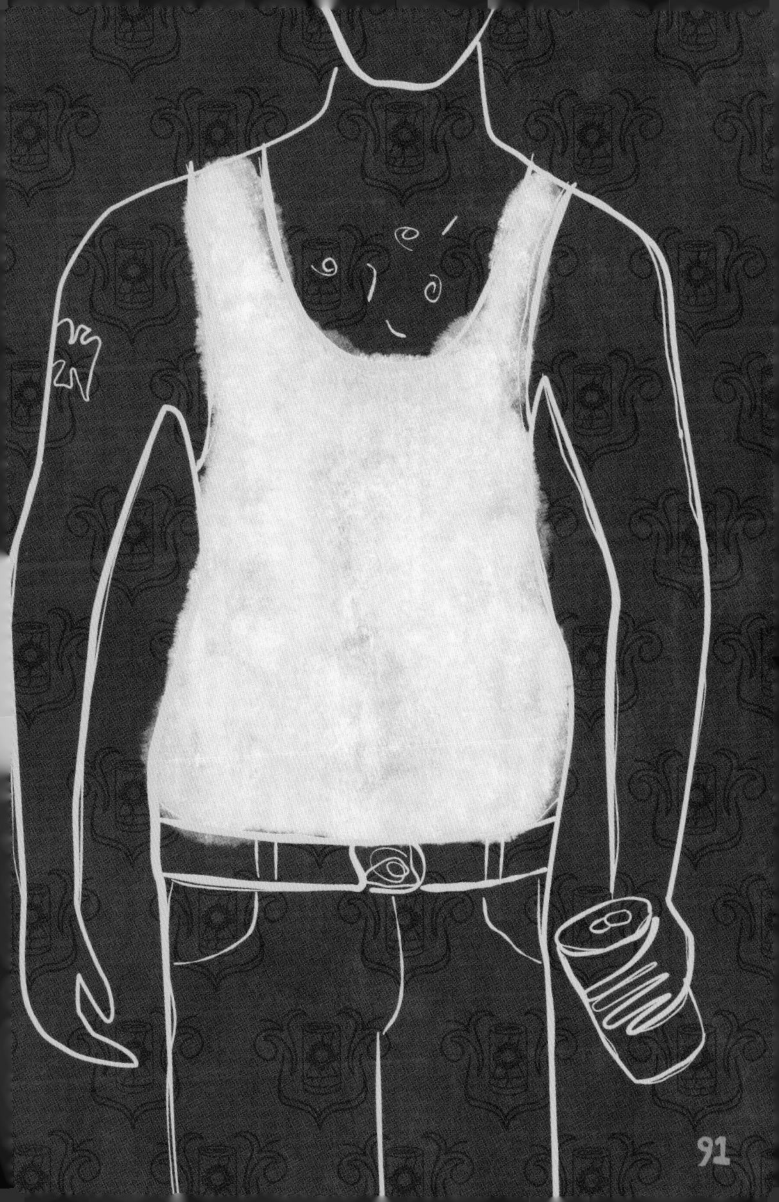

Paparazz
PAPARAZZI
PAPARAZZI

PAPARAZZI
Paparazzi

TRUCKER CAPS
No Fat
Chicks

WET T-SHIRT CONTESTS

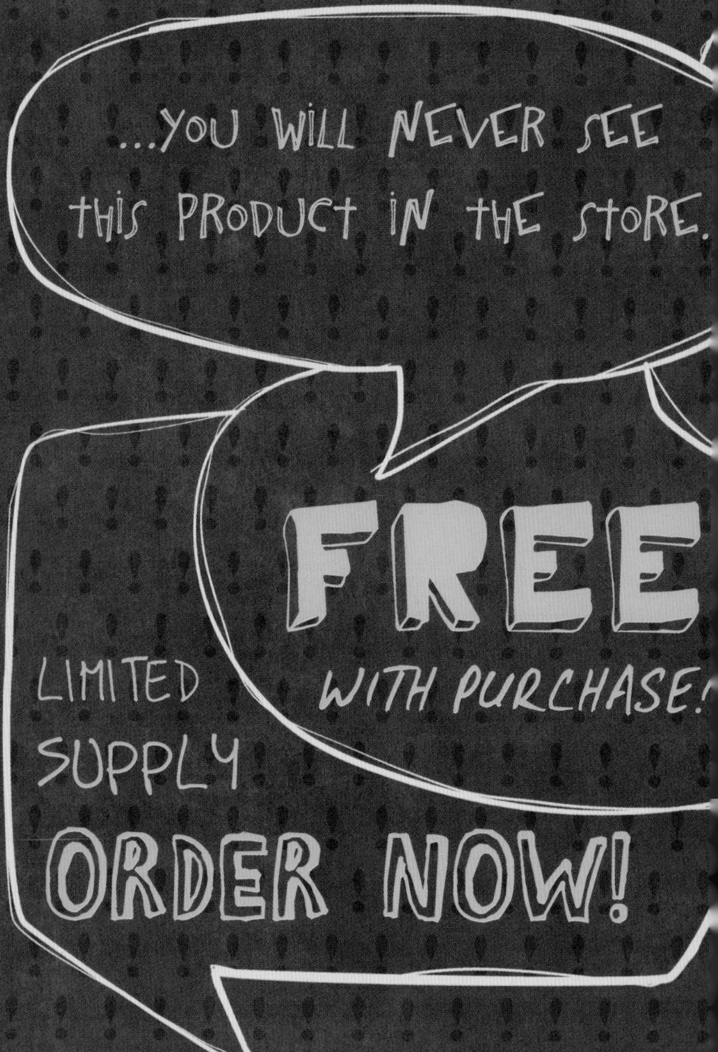
...YOU WILL NEVER SEE
THIS PRODUCT IN THE STORE.
FREE
WITH PURCHASE!
LIMITED
SUPPLY
ORDER NOW!

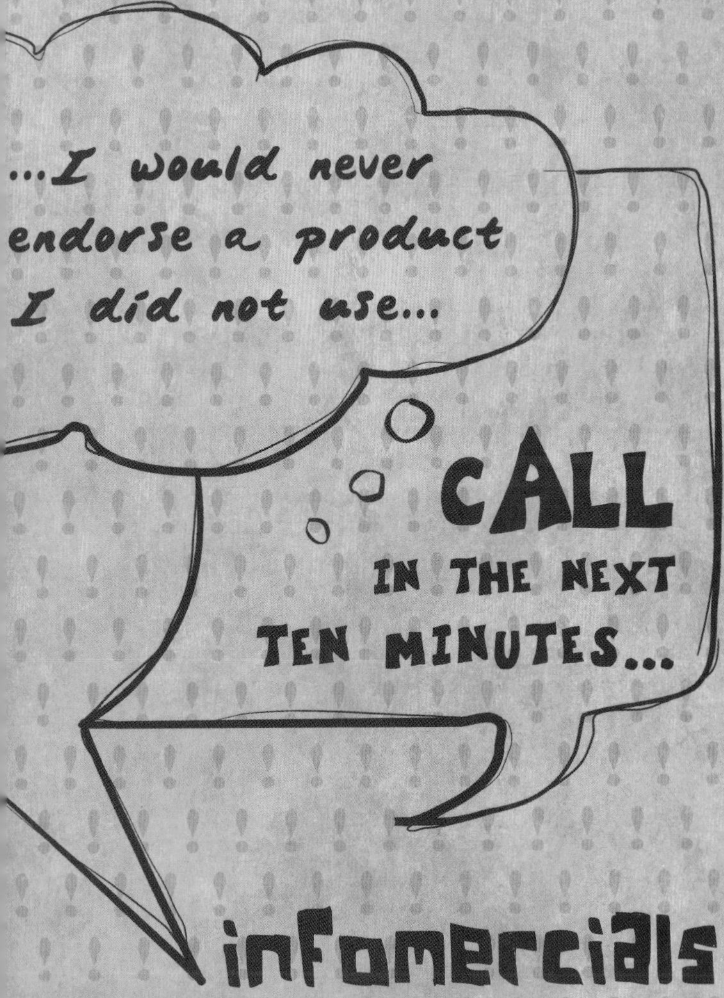

infomercials

COMBOVERS

MULLETS

LOCKER ROOM INTERVIEWS

steroid rage

OVERPAID ATHLETES

Underdressed Cheerleaders

MOVIE SEQUELS

BRIDGET JONES 7:
ANOTHER DATE, ANOTHER DIET

GOATEES

Golf Clothing

COMMITMENT PHOBIA

MAIL-IN REBATES

HELL

PANTYHOSE

QUOTE:

"There are three things that women have to deal with that men don't, which stink. One, periods. Two, bras. Three, pantyhose."

Aimee Kreger Brooks,
New Jersey television producer

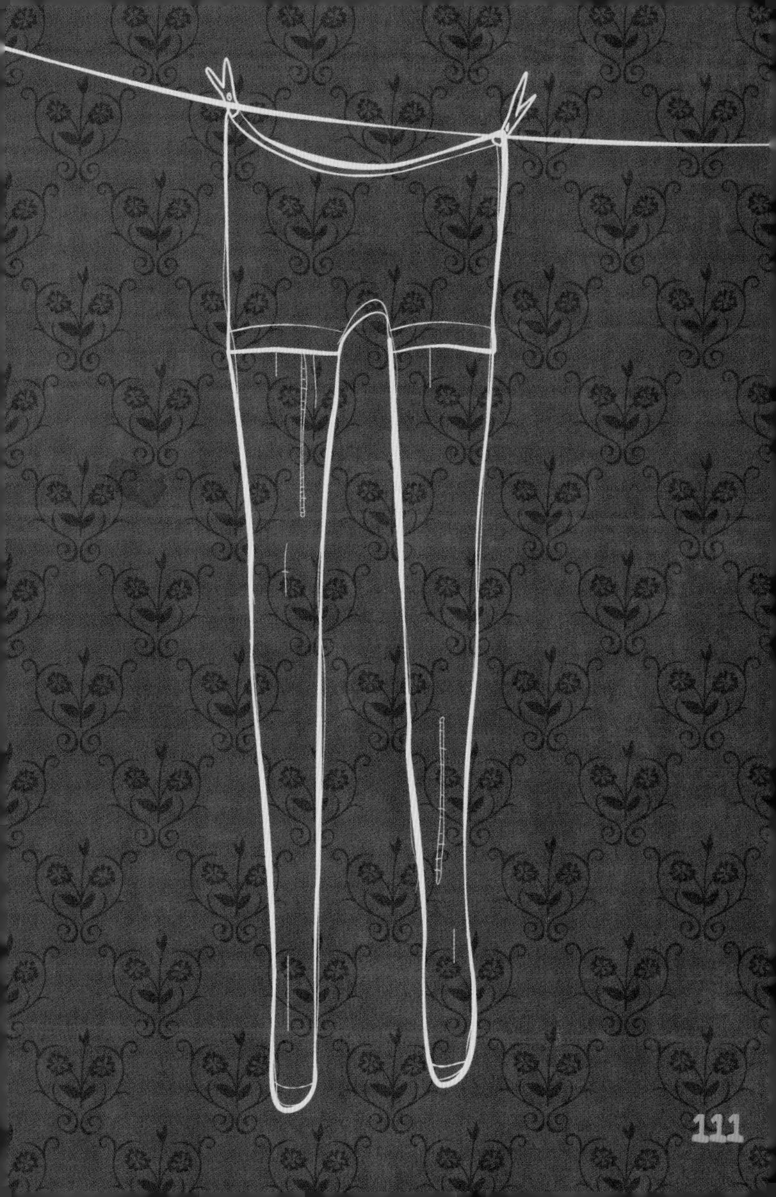

PARKING METERS

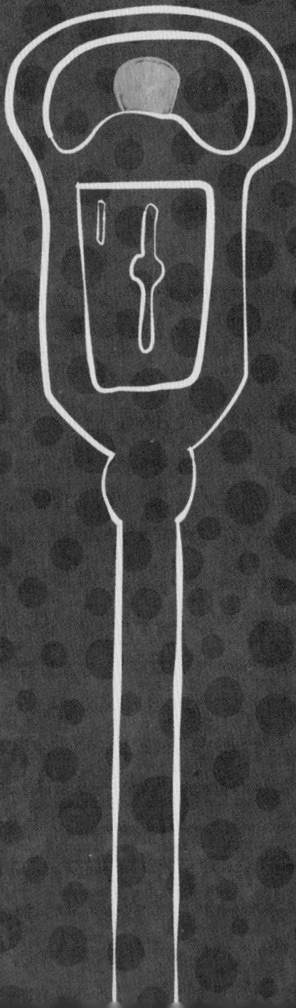

POP-UP INTERNET ADS

Double Standards

Quote

"Easy is an adjective used to describe a woman who has the sexual morals of a man."

-Nancy Linn-Desmond

RAPE

ABERCROMBIE & FITCH ADS

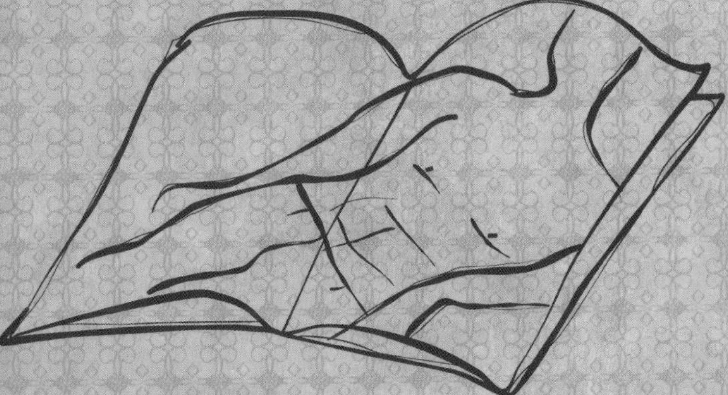

Nikki Hardin is the founder and editor of **skirt!** magazine, a monthly print publication and Web site for women. A native of Kentucky, she left home at seventeen to elope with her high school boyfriend. Twelve years later, divorced with three children and unskilled at almost everything, she started college at the age of twenty-nine. In 1985, she moved to Charleston, South Carolina, where she spent the next several years nursing a midlife crisis while she eked out a living by cleaning houses, working at a bed and breakfast, clerking in a liquor store that had a psychotic parrot, and writing descriptions of mythical Irish pubs for a local mail-order company. She started **skirt!** in 1994 with not much more than $400 and the desire to have something interesting to read.

Caitilin McPhillips grew up in Chevy Chase, Maryland, with four brothers who catered to her every whim—thus, her childhood nickname, The Princess. After graduating from National Cathedral School in Washington, D.C., she convinced her parents that art school was a better educational investment than law school. Armed with a BFA from Kansas City Art Institute, she headed south on the tropical Isle of Palms, just off beautiful Charleston, South Carolina. Many advertisement campaigns later, she met Nikki Hardin, who told her she wanted to start a new magazine—but she had no money and no one to sell the ads. The rest is history. Caitilin lives with her husband and two daughters in the idyllic Old Village section of Mount Pleasant, South Carolina.

SKIRT!
EVE WAS FRAMED

skirt!
is
skirt!
magazine
april 2004
"April, the Angel of the months, the young Love of the year."